D1528021

Gathering
the Bones
Together

Also by Gregory Orr

Burning the Empty Nests

Drawings by Brad Holland

Gathering the Bones Together

GREGORY ORR

HARPER & ROW, PUBLISHERS
NEW YORK, EVANSTON, SAN FRANCISCO, LONDON

The opening sequence of poems entitled "Gathering the Bones Together" appeared in *The American Poetry Review*.

Cold Mountain Press printed a post card of "A Large White Rock Called 'The Sleeping Angel.'"

Other poems in this book, or earlier versions of them appeared in the following magazines: *The Iowa Review, Lamp in the Spine, Paris Review, Poetry Now, Seneca Review, Some*.

GATHERING THE BONES TOGETHER. Copyright © 1975 by Gregory Orr. Illustrations copyright © 1975 by Brad Holland. All rights reserved. Printed in the United States of America. No part of this book may be used or reproduced in any manner whatsoever without written permission except in the case of brief quotations embodied in critical articles and reviews. For information address Harper & Row, Publishers, Inc., 10 East 53rd Street, New York, N.Y. 10022. Published simultaneously in Canada by Fitzhenry & Whiteside Limited, Toronto.

FIRST EDITION

Designed by Gloria Adelson

Library of Congress Cataloging in Publication Data

Orr, Gregory.
  Gathering the bones together.
  I. Title.
PS3565.R7G3   811'.5'4   74–15843
ISBN 0–06–013268–X
ISBN 0–06–013269–8 pbk.

75 76 10 9 8 7 6 5 4 3 2 1

For Trisha

I would like to thank the University of Michigan Society of Fellows whose support was essential to the writing of this book.

G. O.

Contents

1

Gathering the
Bones Together

FOR PETER ORR

When all the rooms of the house
fill with smoke, it's not enough
to say an angel is sleeping on the chimney.

one

A Night in the Barn

The deer carcass hangs from a rafter.
Wrapped in blankets, a boy keeps watch
from a pile of loose hay. Then he sleeps

and dreams about a death that is coming:
Inside him, there are small bones
scattered in a field
among burdocks and dead grass.
He will spend his life walking there,
gathering the bones together.

Pigeons rustle in the eaves.
At his feet, the German shepherd
snaps its jaws in its sleep.

two

A father and his four sons
run down a slope toward
a deer they just killed.
The father and two sons carry
rifles. They laugh, jostle,
and chatter together.
A gun goes off,
and the youngest brother
falls to the ground.
A boy with a rifle
stands beside him, screaming.

three

I crouch in the corner of my room,
staring into the glass well
of my hands; far down
I see him drowning in air.

Outside, leaves shaped like mouths
make a black pool
under a tree. Snails glide
there, little death-swans.

four

Smoke

Something has covered the chimney
and the whole house fills with smoke.
I go outside and look up at the roof,
but I can't see anything.
I go back inside. Everyone weeps,
walking from room to room.
Their eyes ache. This smoke
turns people into shadows.
Even after it is gone, and the tears are gone,
we will smell it in pillows
when we lie down to sleep.

five

He lives in a house of black glass.
Sometimes I visit him, and we talk.
My father says he is dead,
but what does that mean?
Last night I found a child
sleeping on a nest of bones.
He had a red, leaf-shaped
scar on his cheek. I lifted him up
and carried him with me, even though
I didn't know where I was going.

The Journey

Each night, I knelt on a marble slab
and scrubbed at the blood.
I scrubbed for years and still it was there.
But tonight the bones in my feet
begin to burn. I stand up
and start walking, and the slab
appears under my feet with each step,
a white road only as long as your body.

The Distance

The winter I was eight, a horse
slipped on the ice, breaking its leg.
Father took a rifle, a can of gasoline.
I stood by the road at dusk and watched
the carcass burning in the far pasture.

I was twelve when I killed him;
I felt my own bones wrench from my body.
Now I am twenty-seven and walk
beside this river, looking for them.
They have become a bridge
that arches toward the other shore.

2

Weeping he ran to the queen,
and she said, "Who has hurt you?
You were out on the meadow." He
could say nothing, as is still the
way with children.

Parzival, Book Three

Two Lines from the Brothers Grimm

FOR LARRY AND JUDY

Now we must get up quickly,
dress ourselves, and run away.
Because it surrounds us, because
they are coming with wolves on leashes,
because I stood just now at the window
and saw the wall of hills on fire.
They have taken our parents away.
Downstairs in the half dark, two strangers
move about, lighting the stove.

The Hats

The hats are hungry.
What will they eat?
The funny uncle
puts his hand into his hat
and pulls out an empty sleeve.
All the parents are laughing,
but the children are scared.
What will the hats eat now;
the hats our fathers wear?
See the hat in the corner.
Has it been fed?

Child's Song

Father meets you at the water's edge.
He has just dragged
his huge boat up on the beach.
Now he turns
and opens his arms to hug you.

You run along the path by the river.
Mother is coming too; you hear
the soft scissors of her legs
as she chases you
through the woods.

Black Moon

FOR MY MOTHER
(1921–1961)

1
Memories of Haiti

A lizard dozes in the sun,
and a scorpion scratches
about under a rubbish heap.
In the bushes I watch a bird
smaller than a sparrow,
pale green as new leaves.
I am fourteen,
wandering along dusty paths;
brown women squat
naked in a streambed,
pounding their laundry with sticks
and spreading it smooth over stones
to dry. Thick, sweet smell
of rotting mangoes. It is September;
next week my mother
will die, and we will return
to the States, where already
it grows cold.

2
Collapsed Houses

In the woods in upstate New York,
a boy looks for the foundations
of collapsed houses.

17

He digs with his hands
under layers of leaves and soft dirt,
looking for old bottles.
He brings them to his mother,
who washes them in the sink
and puts them on the window sill
where they glow deep green and blue.

Several years later, he stands
at night beside a ruined house.
He kneels by a hole and looks down:
water at the well bottom,
a black moon, his mother's face
floats on its surface.

3
Black Moon

And still it moves through the earth under me
as easily as the other moon
slides through empty space.

The way the white moon pulls
at oceans and blood,
this black moon pulls at my bones.

From That Moment

FOR DOROTHY IRVING

From that moment he breathes more carefully,
like a man who has swallowed a cloud.
It settles in the branches of his lungs.
Although seasons change, the cloud remains.
He grows older and still
he spends a part of each day
standing at the foot of the tree
gazing up at its mysterious guest.

Before We Met

FOR TRISHA

1

You lived with eight sisters
in a warm ocean;
the bottom half of your body
was a transparent stalk
rooted in sand.
But all that sailors saw
was a beautiful woman
calling from the water.

2

Later you slept beside that ocean,
and with a seashell of hair
held to your ear
you listened to the dead.
Wind whistled at little holes
in the transparent statue of a woman
standing a few feet away.
Through these same holes, sand
entered, slowly filling her body.

3

You dreamt of me,
and on the wall above my bed,
a thin crack appeared:

20

out of it crawled blue moths.
They clustered together in the air,
wings beating, making a kind of blue sun.

4

I woke. I started walking
toward you on this bridge
of poems: a thousand
paper coffins
laid end to end.

5

On the cave walls,
you were pasting pictures
of the moon's phases.

I sat by the entrance,
waiting, a heart-shaped
stone in my lap.

Other men waded naked
where the waves rose and fell,
fishing with baskets.

6

We lay together in the sand at dawn.
Far out over the ocean
angels rode shoreward on their tall clouds
and green fish spread their wings.

7

Like any other man

I was born with a knife
in one hand
and a wound in the other.

In the house where I lived
all the mirrors
were painted black.

So many years
before the soft key of your tongue
unlocked my body.

3

A Life

At dawn you curl up in the top branches
and sleep.
All day you are a cloud.
Birds fly through it.

At dusk animals gather at the waterhole
as if to drink, but it has become a mirror,
because you are dreaming:

                  At your feet
glass has replaced water, the way
words have replaced feeling.

All night you sit in the tree, listening
to the howl and moan of the animals
in the darkness below.

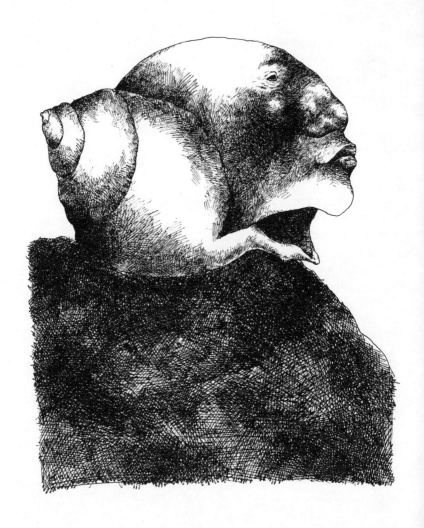

The Teeth of Sleep

Dragon jaws close over your head;
next morning you wake up wearing
a little necklace of blood pearls.

The Spider

Each night since my mother died
I sit at the table
while the spider spins her web.
She goes over it again and again,
until each strand is thick and soft.
When the web is finished, the spider
shrinks. She is exhausted.
I slip my hands carefully
into the web's empty spaces,
lift it like gray yarn
and carry it into the kitchen.

The Snail

The snail sat in the blind man's palm.
The man remembered Helen Keller's dream:
that she held a pearl in her hand,
and she "saw" it,
the most beautiful thing in her life.
"What is a snail?" the blind man asked.
It is a pearl that dies.
You can find its empty shell
at the foot of a tree in the woods
like a white ear that is listening.

The Cage

After its capture, the animal
was caged in a room of mirrors.
Staring at itself, it began
to shed great clumps of fur.
To save itself, it learned
to close its left eye,
hiding that half of its body.
Its right side shriveled up,
but its left hand
seized things and continued to grow.

A Large White Rock Called
"The Sleeping Angel"

He lay down in this field to rest.
Seeing an ant carry
a white egg the size of a rice grain,
the angel believed it was a sign
that the animals of this world
wanted to make him their king.
While he slept, sheep licked
his salt wings.
Only these stubs remain.

The Transformation

At night the house fills with seawater,
and you become a gigantic turtle.
You slip off your bed and the weight
of your shell pulls you deeper, down through
the house toward the basement
where you drift above a forest of coral.
Moving your head from side to side,
you search for the egg buried under mud.
You find it, scoop it into your mouth
and begin to rise up the stairs,
stroking slowly,
the way a man breathes in his sleep.

The King of the Earthworms

Waking each day, always at the end
of a tunnel,
dirt pressed against my face,
I move by taking a bite,
chewing my way through the packed rubble
of earth, roots, and bones.
Like Chuang-tzu's butterfly, I cherish
an alternate life: that of a man
who lies down to sleep;
one wall of his room disappears
and the mattress floats out
into the night air.

4

The Man in the Suit of Mirrors

FOR STANLEY AND ELISE

1
To the Man in the Suit of Mirrors

You stand with the sun behind you,
and your suit shines with red light.

Or you are lying asleep under the tree
at the field's edge, like a pool of still water
that appears suddenly at our feet.

2
His Room

The man in the suit of mirrors
lives in an empty room.
He has only the one suit.
He sleeps in the center of the floor,
the suit hanging over him
like a chandelier, a tree of cold light.

3
His Passing

Before he passes, the stones shine
with a white light of their own.
After, they become heavy and gray.
He walks through the fields in his suit
of mirrors. In one hand, he carries
a small black pillow.

In the other he holds a skull:
the bone has opened at the sutures
and spread like thick petals.

4
Parable of His Origins

As though his parents were two mirrors
and an anger, silent as light,
passed back and forth between them.

5
An Evening at Home

The man in the suit of mirrors
enters my yard. Holding a lantern
in one hand, he pounds
on my door with his fist.
I don't come out. I crouch
down in the dust like a mouse.

6
The Hill

In the clear air of morning,
I follow him up a steep path.
His suit gleams in the sunlight;
I stare instead at his feet
that leave no print, even in this soft earth.

We climb past trees whose leaves
are covered with flies;
a breeze sends them trailing out
like banners of smoke.

At the top of the hill I meet my mother,
much older than when she died.
She smiles. She is sewing
feathers onto a white shirt.
I unwind the long bandage of my skin
and step out: a gray, man-shaped cloud.

5

And so I went home to my bed and
left him to pick his way through
the mud and darkness to Brighton,
or Bright-town, which he will reach
some time in the morning.

THOREAU, *Walden*

The Dead in Early Spring

It is that time when last year's dead,
healed by their brief sleep,
rise up through thawing ground,
gather in small bands, and enter
the woods to begin their new lives.
Under the budless trees, they will build
their huts out of mud and bones.
We watch as they pick their way
among the last few bandages of snow
at the field's edge.

The Nocturnal Picnic

The parents mutter about almost being
murdered by owls and bats; the children
hug large red stones to their chests
to hold them down. In the woods
behind them, leaves are moving
although there is no wind.
They seem tired and glad it's over, as
they walk at dawn through the wet meadow,
carrying their empty baskets.

Moving to the City

Struggling to open
a very important package,
a young man
stabbed himself in the palm.
That night leaves turned black,
people walked on four legs
and ate ice,
his mother's ear became a gold coin.
When the man woke
the next day, these things
remained the same.

The Abandoned Garden

Leafless trees, dry plant stalks; I am in a garden surrounded by smooth high walls decorated with murals of autumn gardens: stagnant green ponds and scarlet maples. Suddenly I realize I am standing in the empty snail shell I found yesterday in the woods. This shell must be the same one Georg Trakl lived in, before he was run over from behind by one of the first German tanks.

The Project

My plan was to generate light
with no outside source.
To accomplish this, I lived alone
in a burrow under the earth.
Previously I had observed
that in darkness my body
gave off a faint light. Suspecting
that this glow came from the bones,
I scraped the flesh from my right hand.
I'd been underground so long
the meat came off
painlessly, like wet clay.
But when the flesh was gone,
the light was gone too.

A House in the Country

FOR DON AND JANE

1
The Field

In my last lifetime, I was
the large mushroom growing
over a corpse in the woods.

In this, I stand at dusk in fields,
cast my shadow out over the grass,
watch as it settles, then
pull it toward me.
Mice and song sparrows
are tangled in it,
and these I eat.

2
The Coat

I still have a coat my father
gave me; a huge, stiff thing
made of horsehide.
His grandfather
made it from his favorite horse,
because when the horse died
he wouldn't let it go.

3
Overtaken by Fog While Climbing Mt. Chikora,
New Hampshire

The path at my feet disappears
in thick mist.
I sit down on a rock and wait.
To pass the time, I stare
at my hand floating
far away at the end of its sleeve
like a white plant root;
it doesn't seem attached
even to its own wrist.
It is hard to love this thing,
so frail and alien.

4
Finding a Snail in the Woods

You made it yourself:
this little shellhouse
you carry on your back.
When you die, it will
become your tombstone,
just as this poem will be mine.

Someone
walking in the woods
will pick it up
and know that you once lived.

The Survival Gardens

I work in the gardens, hoeing
and thinning the vegetable rows.
At night, the mouths
of those who starved that day
appear at my bedside.
After each has kissed me
lightly on the cheek,
I wake up. I see them:
two rows across the floor
and out into the darkness:
hoofprints of a horse
that gallops over the earth.

The Sweater

I will lose you. It is written
into this poem the way
the fisherman's wife knits
his death into the sweater.

These Words

1
Night Walk

Under my boots
the earth is bone.
I look up;
against the gray sky,
a bat flies
its centerless dance:
it is these words,
a dark little poem
with no heart.

2
The Shadow-Coffin

How many times, glancing
in hall mirrors, I saw it
hovering a few feet behind me.

And I wanted to turn
and open it, like
a door in the air.

3

All day I climb
the muddy stairs.
Around my neck, inside
the heart-shaped locket:
an ivory mouse.

Sometimes I think a mirror
is a window into another room,
and sometimes a picture covers
ragged holes through which
a black wind blows.

4

Inside me:
a tiny, transparent double.
Each night I dream, it grows
a little larger. One morning
it will fill my body;
its glass face
become my face.

5

In sleep, my body is a branch
and the guardian descends:
owl with wet, red claws.

6

Small animals gnaw
at my ankles.
Hands at my sides,
heavy with the weight
of things.

Again I leave my bones
like a pile of clothes, folded
at the foot of a tree.
A blue light grows
like fur from my body.

Above, on a dead branch,
the owl sits:
dinner-plate face, flat and round;
its yellow beak
closed on a mouse.

6

The Builders

FOR TRISHA

Midnight: the field becomes white stone.
We quarry it. We carry the cut squares
strapped to our backs.

On the side of a bleak hill
we build our hut; windowless,
but filled with light.

Pastoral

1

The others thought you were dead,
so they left your body under a tree
and continued their journey.
But you were alive.
Overhead the years passed
like huge animals crossing a field.

2

You woke in a windowless room.
Plant roots dangled from the ceiling
like frayed ropes.
You saw yourself lying on the floor
asleep, almost transparent.
A white fox watched you
from a tangle of roots in the corner;
a blue flame moved above its head.

3

The moon rose white and full,
as you wandered through a field
of abandoned furniture.
On the other side of the valley, farmers
were making the clouds into trees.
But when you got there
everyone was gone except the woman
who swallowed the children.

When she opened her mouth to scream,
they ran out.
By the time she closed her mouth,
they were all gone.
They were hidden in the trees.

4

For a long time you felt your way
through darkness, crawling on all fours,
emerged at last in a plowed field,
mouth full of dirt. You dug
a little hole with a pointed stick.
What seeped in you didn't drink;
instead you waited while muddy water
grew to a pond. On its surface
empty milkweed pods
drifted like the luminous hulls
of rowboats.

5

You sit in a chair in the middle of the road.
It is raining large, green drops
that do not break.
A blind man approaches,
pounding his cane on the street.
You give him all your clothes
and a bone
carved as a rose.

All Morning

All morning the dream lingers.
I am like thick grass
in a meadow, still
soaked with dew at noon.

Domestic Life

1
Today

Open yourself up: today
that's no different than opening
a refrigerator door: large chunks
of meat, eggs
scattered on the metal racks,
and cowering in the back:
a tiny, frightened woman.
You are huge and clumsy;
you fumble for her, breaking
all the eggs, and she eludes you,
and you don't feel a thing
except cold inside.

2
Something

Something is burning inside you
like a rose made from cellophane,
like something white burning
in a snowfield: no flames,
all you can see is the shadow
of smoke on the snow.

3

Before Dawn

Your wife left before you woke.
She scratched a note on your back;
you try to read it with mirrors.

You decide to talk to the cat,
but when you open your mouth
honey-colored wasps fly out.

The blood in the light bulbs
burns less brightly.

4

The Waterfall

Failing to hold on to things,
a man can become
a waterfall. His friends
stare, silent and aghast,
as he disappears
over the cliff, carrying
off his books, his wife,
all his furniture.

5

Fall Cleaning

This morning, the almost weightless bodies
of insects drift down
from the ceiling. It's seasonal;

you have to expect that sort of thing
when you live in a burrow under the earth.
Yesterday a package arrived
in the mail; it contained bird beaks
in assorted colors and sizes.
Some are small like yellow thorns,
but others are larger;
I slip those over my fingers,
clack them together and dance
around the room in my gray bathrobe.
The insects revive. I am their god.
They dance after me up the tunnel
and out into the autumn woods.